POSTER CO...

REVUE 1926

Mit einem Essay von/Essay by Hans Ulrich Gumbrecht

Herausgegeben von/Edited by Felix Studinka

MUSEUM FÜR GESTALTUNG ZÜRICH
PLAKATSAMMLUNG/POSTER COLLECTION

LARS MÜLLER PUBLISHERS

1 **Carl Moos**
Davos/All the World's Sport Centre

VORWORT

Gegenstände transportieren Geschichten. Nach allen erdenklichen Kriterien gefiltert, systematisiert und mit immer deutlicher werdenden Absichten hinterlegt, werden sie als Zeugen ihrer Zeit weitergereicht und zu einer Masse gefügt, aus der dann «Geschichte» geschrieben wird. Der institutionalisierte Versuch, sich mit materieller Dauer dem Strom des Vergessens entgegenzustemmen, ist die Domäne der Bibliotheken, Archive und Sammlungen. Seit Jahrzehnten spezialisiert sich das Museum für Gestaltung Zürich auf ein Medium, das besonders flüchtig ist: Plakate. Seine Plakatsammlung bildet einen gewaltigen Speicher, der die internationale Geschichte des Plakats belegt und der kontinuierlich ausgebaut und aktualisiert wird. Die neue Publikationsreihe, deren erste Nummer Sie in den Händen halten, ist angelegt als Bestandeskatalog, der diese Sammlung etappenweise bekannt machen und zugleich auch ihre Praxis des Sammelns zur Diskussion stellen soll.

Die Kriterien der Plakatsammlung gründen nicht nur auf ästhetischen Überlegungen, sondern auch auf der Eigenschaft des Plakats als Zeitdokument. Das traditionelle Konzept einer Sammlung von Meisterwerken ist von jenem eines visuellen Archivs nicht zu trennen. Erst die Charakterisierung der Plakatsammlung als komplexes Geflecht, das viele Brennpunkte und Tiefenschärfen zulässt, das Meisterhafte ebenso zu seinem Recht kommen lässt wie das Triviale, umschreibt die ideale Bedingung, unter der sie die Plakatgeschichte wiedergeben will.

Die Nähe zu den Ablagerungen des Alltags haben uns für Hans Ulrich Gumbrechts Buch «1926 – Ein Jahr am Rand der Zeit»[1] empfänglich gemacht. In der Spielart einer Enzyklopädie hat der Autor eine Studie über die Repräsentation von Geschichte anhand konkreten Quellenmaterials geschrieben, wobei er den Zeitraum seiner Untersuchung auf das zufällig gewählte Jahr 1926 beschränkt hat. Warum 1926? Im allgemeinen Urteil kommt dieser Zeitspanne keine nennenswerte Bedeutung zu. Aber gerade darum bot es sich an, sie in ihrer ungefilterten Rohform greifbar werden zu lassen. Der Anspruch bestand darin, Geschichte nicht als bedeutungsschwere, folgerichtige Kette von Ereignissen zu erzählen, sondern als Schauplatz der Gleichzeitigkeit erfahrbar zu machen. Gumbrecht hat die Fahrstühle, Fliessbänder, Ozeandampfer und Grammophone von 1926 wieder in Bewegung gesetzt, hat seine Akteure auf eine Bühne gebeten, in deren Licht ihre Unscheinbarkeit interessant wurde. Wenn es ihm darum ging, die historische Umgebung von 1926 mit grösster Unmittelbarkeit Revue passieren zu lassen, ohne zu versuchen, sie zu interpretieren oder zu verstehen, so hat er damit auch jene sinnliche Realität erzeugt, die Archive auszeichnet. Der Versuch, den literarischen Spuren von Gumbrechts Buch eine visuelle Spur beizufügen, schien naheliegend. Nicht zuletzt auch darum, weil sich eine Sammlung, die sich als «kollektives Gedächtnis» legitimiert, die von Gumbrecht aufgeworfene Frage vor Augen halten muss, was man sich unter «Vergangenheit» als Rohmaterial überhaupt vorzustellen hat. Vor allem aber, um Sie an der Freude teilhaben zu lassen, zu entdecken, wie sich die Merkmale eines Zeitraums in seinen Plakaten offenbaren.

Felix Studinka

1 Hans Ulrich Gumbrecht, *In 1926. Living at the Edge of Time,* Harvard University Press, Cambridge (Massachusetts) / London 1997. *1926 – Ein Jahr am Rand der Zeit,* Suhrkamp Verlag Frankfurt am Main 2001.

FOREWORD

Objects tell stories. They are filtered according to all conceivable criteria, systematized and set aside with a purpose that becomes ever clearer, passed on as evidence of their time, and then finally assembled as a mass that is used to write "history". Institutionalizing the attempt to brace oneself against the flood of forgetfulness by turning to the durability of materials is the domain of archives, libraries and collections. For decades now, the Museum für Gestaltung Zürich has been specializing in a medium that is particularly ephemeral: posters. Its poster collection forms a valuable storehouse for the international history of the poster, and this is being actively expanded. This new series of publications, the first one of which you are holding in your hands, is designed as an inventory catalogue intended to make the collection known in stages, and at the same time to stimulate discussion about the way in which the collection has been put together.

The criteria of the poster collection are not just derived from aesthetic considerations, but also from the poster's quality as a document of its times. Therefore the traditional concept of a collection of masterpieces is not to be separated from that of a visual archive. It is only when a poster collection is seen as a complex tissue of material that admits a large number of focal points and focal depths, allowing the avant-garde as much scope as peripheral scenes of visual communication, that the ideal conditions are established for the history of posters to unfold.

Closeness to the deposits laid down by everyday life made us receptive to the idea behind Hans Ulrich Gumbrecht's book "In 1926. Living at the Edge of Time".[1] Gumbrecht used encyclopaedia-style approach to write a study of the representation of history using concrete source material, restricting himself entirely to the randomly chosen year of 1926 for the period of his investigations. Why 1926? The general view is that this period had no particular significance. But precisely because it doesn't occupy a key position, it seemed a good idea to make it tangible in its untreated raw form. The aim was not to narrate history as a highly significant, logical chain of events, but to lay it open to experience as a confused accumulation of simultaneous events. Gumbrecht set the lifts, conveyor belts, ocean liners and gramophones of 1926 in motion again, and asked his actors to step on to a stage whose lighting made their unspectacular nature into something interesting. He intended to conjure up the historic environment of 1926, to review it as directly as possible, without trying to interpret or understand it, but he also succeeded in creating the kind of sensual reality that is a quality of archives. His provocatively uninhibited, superficial perception of source material inspired us to add a visual strand made up of the posters of the day to the literary strands from which he wove his book. And this was also because a collection that justifies itself as a "collective memory" has to keep its eye on the question Gumbrecht raised about how we should understand the "past" as raw material in the first place. But above all wanted to let you share the delight of discovering how the characteristics of a period of time are revealed in its posters.

Felix Studinka

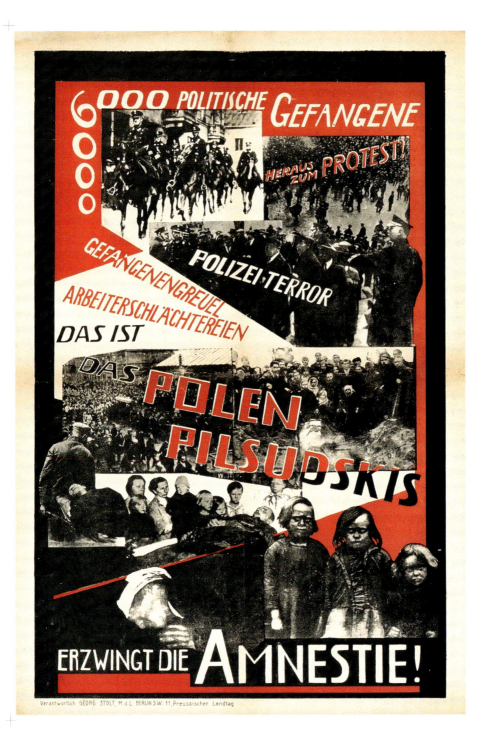

2 **Anonym**
6000 politische Gefangene/Das ist das Polen
Pilsudskis/Erzwingt die Amnestie!
6000 political prisoners/This is Pilsudski's
Poland/Force an amnesty!

3 **Anonym**
Stern Brothers present Buster's Mix-up

4 **Herbert Bayer**
Kandinsky Jubiläums-Ausstellung zum 60. Geburtstag
Kandinsky's 60th birthday anniversary exhibition

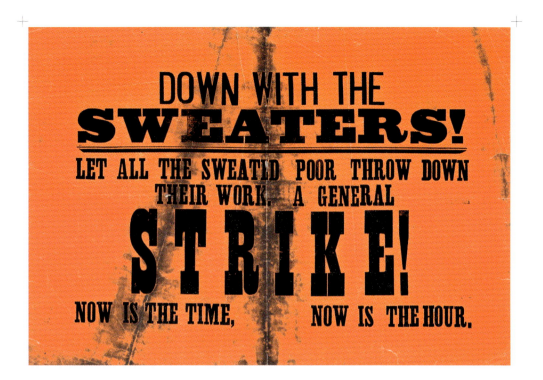

5 **Anonym**
Down with the sweaters! A general strike!
Nieder mit den Ausbeutern! Generalstreik!

6 **Marcello Nizzoli**
F N (Fabrique Nationale)

7 **Otto Morach**
Der Weg zur Kraft u. Gesundheit führt über Davos
The way to strength and health is via Davos

EIN JAHR ALS UMGEBUNG

Hans Ulrich Gumbrecht

Jeden Tag war es mein Traum, in den Monaten als ich das Buch «1926 – Ein Jahr am Rand der Zeit» schrieb, dass dieses Jahr zu einer Umgebung würde. Etwas genauer gesagt: Die Idealvorstellung, der ich mit einem Text näher kommen wollte, ohne ganz naiv die dem Medium «Text» gesetzten Wirkungsgrenzen zu übersehen, war die Vorstellung vom Jahr 1926 als einem Raum, durch den man würde gehen können. Das war am Anfang gar nicht mehr als eine Konkretisierung und als die Intensivierung jener alten Metapher des «sich Versenkens» in eine vergangene Welt. Und solches «mich Versenken» hat schon immer so sehr zu meinen Lieblingsbeschäftigungen gehört, dass ich mich inzwischen zu der Überzeugung verstiegen habe, die Faszina-tion des «sich Versenkens» sei eine gemeinsame Grundlage für all die verschiedenen Ausprägungen von – akademischen und nichtakademischen – Formen historischer Kultur. Aus-der-Geschichte-Lernen und Geschichtsphilosophie, Archäologie und Antiken-Sammeln, historische Romane und Historienmalerei, all diese Praktiken set-zen, glaube ich, die primäre Faszination eines «sich Versenkens» in die Vergangenheit voraus, und sie beziehen aus ihr Inspiration und Energie.

Ohne dass ich selbst zunächst auch nur eine Sekunde an die Verwirklichung meines Traumes gedacht oder gar geglaubt hätte, ist er nun in der Ausstellung der Plakat-sammlung des Museums für Gestaltung wirklich geworden – und indem man durch die zu einer Umgebung, zu einem Raum gewordenen Erinnerung an das Jahr 1926 gehen kann, hat sich – paradoxerweise – das Maximum dessen eingelöst, was ich für das Buch über 1926 zu hoffen nie gewagt hatte. Ich meine das – trotz der paradoxen Formulierung – in einem ganz präzisen Sinn, welcher nicht zuletzt der Sinn einer Negation ist. Denn mein Buch – und auch diese Ausstellung – würden missverstan-den, wenn man versuchte, ihnen so etwas wie ein «tieferes Verstehen» des Jahres 1926 abzugewinnen. Das Jahr tiefer oder auch nur besser verstehen zu wollen, hiesse ja einerseits, es mit jenen ihm vorausgehenden Handlungen und Bewegungen zu assoziieren, aus denen das Jahr 1926 hervorgegangen sein mochte; und es bedeutete andererseits auch, das Jahr mit jenen Folgeentwicklungen zusammen-zubringen, für die wir es als den Moment «historischer Weichenstellung» ansehen könnten. Aus der Absicht, *ein Jahr zu verstehen,* folgt also, wie wir sehen, über-raschenderweise vielleicht, dass man sich *gerade nicht primär auf dieses Jahr selbst konzentriert;* und eine solche, über ein in Frage stehendes Jahr hinausreichende Perspektive bringt dann ganz unvermeidlich auch die Aufgabe mit sich, ein «bedeut-sames Jahr», ein «Schwellenjahr» für die historische Arbeit auszuwählen, ein Jahr, aus dem sich möglichst viel Vorausgehendes und möglichst viel Folgendes erklären lassen soll. Gewiss ist solches Verstehen immer noch wichtig und ohnehin legitim – aber es war doch nie Teil des Traums, den ich mit meinem Buch verband und den nun diese Ausstellung verwirklicht. Ich wollte nämlich *bloss die Oberflächen des Jahres 1926,* seine Töne, Gefühle und Gerüche, seine Formen, Farben und Umrisse *auf meine*

Sinne wirken lassen – und dies nicht etwa deshalb, weil ich diesem Jahr irgendeine besondere Bedeutsamkeit zugeschrieben hätte. Meine ganze – wissenschaftlich durchaus problematische – Motivation bestand darin, dass ich lange genug geglaubt hatte, zwei meiner Grosseltern seien 1926 gestorben, um so etwas wie eine spezifische 1926-Begierde zu entwickeln.

Wer sich auf diese Weise in den Raum einer Umgebung aus Vergangenheit versenkt, der wird entdecken, dass sich vielerlei Formen und Themen in dieser Umgebung bald wiederholen – und zwar in überraschender Weise wiederholen. Nicht weniges von dem, was man auf den ersten, zweiten und dritten Blick registriert, kehrt nicht nur immer wieder, sondern kehrt wieder in immer neuen Kontexten und Rekombinationen, deren Abfolge sich nicht auf irgendeine Formel bringen lässt. Das genau, das unvorhersehbare, aber unablässige Auftauchen solcher Rekurrenzen, macht am Ende die Identität eines Zeitraums aus, in den man sich versenkt (ohne ihn eigentlich verstehen zu wollen). Vor zwanzig oder mehr Jahren, als die Semiotik auf den Chefetagen der Geisteswissenschaftler und des Kulturmanagements noch hoch im Theorie-Kurs stand, hätte man wohl versucht, einen solchen Eindruck und Befund durch den Ansatz zu einer «Grammatik» des entsprechenden kulturgeschichtlichen Moments zu systematisieren. Es wäre damals der Ehrgeiz der Kulturwissenschaftler und Kulturprofis gewesen, den Oberflächeneindruck der Ausstellungsbesucher mit einer «tieferen Einsicht» zu übertrumpfen. Heute sind wir, hoffe ich, etwas gelassener geworden. Genau wie die Ausstellungsbesucher (mit dem Unterschied nur, dass wir uns mehr Zeit dabei nehmen dürfen und im Regelfall dafür sogar bezahlt werden) erfolgen wir Kulturwissenschaftler geduldig und wachsend fasziniert solche wiederkehrenden Formen und Themen eines historischen Zeitraums – als eine unvorhersehbare Sequenz, welche sich nicht auf eine Formel bringen lassen wird, aber doch beständig an Dichte und Intensität gewinnt. Wir verfolgen sie als das, was die französischen Philosophen Gilles Deleuze und Félix Guattari einmal «Rhizom» genannt haben: als ein Geflecht von Affinitäten und Assoziationen, das weder endlos noch scharf umschrieben ist, weder lückenlos noch diskontinuierlich.

Vielleicht entdecken ja auch Sie bei der Betrachtung der Plakate zuallererst (so ging es mir vor einigen Jahren), dass es 1926 so etwas wie eine *Kopfbedeckungs-Besessenheit* gab. Aber niemand sprach natürlich damals von einer Besonderheit oder einem durchgängigen Symptom. Warum hat der kleine Junge im Vordergrund des Plakats für den Film Buster's Mix-Up 3 so eine ausladende Matrosenmütze, und was ist es, das sich um den Kopf des Mädchens zu seiner Rechten rankt? Eine Protoform von Micky-Mouse-Ohren vielleicht? Besser gewöhnen Sie sich möglichst bald daran, dass es auf solche Warum-Fragen kaum einmal eine Antwort gibt, und lassen sich stattdessen besser, wenn Sie Ihren Entdeckerspass an den gezeigten Plakaten haben wollen, darauf ein, frei zwischen Ihren Beobachtungen zu assoziieren, um dann in solch freiem Beobachten Serien von strukturellen Affinitäten zu entdecken. Dabei wird Ihnen wahrscheinlich auffallen, dass der den Staat darstellende Fettwanst auf dem Aufruf gegen die öffentliche «Wohnungsbau-Initiative» von 1926 64 eine Landsknechtskappe mit riesigem Federbusch trägt, und dass kaum eine der von griechisch-antiken Formen inspirierten Gestalten, welche Ihnen so oft begegnen werden, je ihr Haar zeigt. Sie haben den Helm des Botschaftergottes Hermes mit seinen kleinen Flügeln aufgesetzt oder antike Soldatenhelme mit halblangen Visieren, die Kopfbedeckung der Pallas-Athene mit vielfachen Emblemen der Weisheit 38 – oder auch, ganz anachronistisch, jene Phyrgiermütze welche schon seit der Revolution im späten 18. Jahrhundert das Haupt der Marianne, Frankreichs Allegorie, geschmückt hatte. Wenn Sie denn wirklich einmal Haar zu sehen bekommen, ist es extrem stilisiert; vor allem zu einem Bubikopf (dem *bobbed hair* im amerikanischen Englisch jener Zeit), zu jener eng anliegenden, immer schwarz vorgestellten Jungenfrisur, welche die geometrisch geschnittenen Kleider unterstreicht, in denen weibliche Körperformen so leicht verschwinden. Selbst auf den Bildern aus der sonst frugalen Sowjetunion entdeckt man aber auch das andere Extrem: ins Frauenhaar geflochtene Turbane, welche in Strähnen ausufern und dann wie die Strähnen der Furcht erregenden Medusa (oder wie die Fühler eines überdimensionalen Insekts) den Raum um den jeweiligen Kopf zu explorieren scheinen 76.

Lassen Sie sich und Ihre Imagination also anstecken von einer vergangenen Entdeckerfreude, von der Freude an dem 1926 wohl grenzenlos wirkenden Experiment, «natürliche» Formen und Lagen des menschlichen Körpers «künstlich» und in allen vorstellbaren Richtungen zu variieren und zu verändern. Frauen auf der Höhe der Mode wollten wirken wie adoleszente Männer, und die Männer hatten seit dem 17. Jahrhundert nie mehr so viel Make-up benutzt wie in den zwanziger Jahren (ist Ihnen jemals aufgefallen, dass selbst Thomas Mann Rouge auflegte?) Körper mit lebenden Ornamenten zu drapieren war eine ästhetische Passion im Variété und im Zirkus jener Welt 1, 17, 19, 55. Solcher Spass am Experimentieren mit der Veränderbarkeit dessen, was eben noch natürlich erschienen war, entwickelte sich durchaus auch zu einem politischen Stil. Dies war die Zeit, in der sich Pädagogen und Reformpolitiker mit Vorliebe «Sozial-Ingenieure» nannten. Als ein solch anscheinend grenzenloses Planungs-Projekt fortschrittlichster Sozial-Ingenieure faszinierte die Sowjetunion nicht nur die Intellektuellen von 1926 8, 75. Nie, fürchte ich, sind soziale Hierarchien weniger als unveränderbares Schicksal erfahren worden als damals: kein Streik-Ziel schien unerreichbar und keine Statistik, keine Selbstdarstellung, kein Reisebericht aus dem ehemals russischen Arbeiter- und Bauernparadies klang zu optimistisch, um ernstgenommen zu werden 32, 80. Eine Trivialversion der symmetrischen Träume von der neuen Gesellschaft war der Hygiene-Furor, welcher gerade die europäische Mittelklasse überfallen hatte 77. Bubikopf, Charleston-Kleid und ein kleiner häuslicher Ehrgeiz, den strahlend-saubersten Spülstein zu haben, standen sich keinesfalls im Weg.
Falls es Ihnen nicht als historisches Faktum vertraut ist, können Sie es an den gezeigten Plakaten fast ohne Abstriche *live* erleben: Während der Generalstreik

der englischen Bergbauarbeiter im Jahr 1926 scheiterte 5 und während wir die Sowjetunion heute längst als das am katastrophalsten gescheiterte Experiment der Menschheitsgeschichte klassifiziert haben, verdanken wir den zwanziger Jahren immerhin die allgemeine Erwartung und das allgemein verbriefte Recht auf *Ferien*. Exuberante italienische Strände 15, das romantische Mittelgebirge in Belgien 44 und die majestätischen Schweizer Alpen 45–47 waren mit einem Mal nicht mehr bloss Motiv für die Maler, Beschreibungsgegenstand der Geographen und Herausforderung für einige wenige Sportler. In der Vorstellung der Zeitgenossen waren sie alle zu Orten der Ruhe, Entspannung und Rekreation geworden, zu Räumen, die sich den Körpern derer öffneten, die hart und fast ununterbrochen gearbeitet hatten. Sollte wahre Politik allerdings tatsächlich die «Kunst des Möglichen» sein, dann waren Ferien – eher als die radikalen Utopien von der ganz neuen Gesellschaft – die eigentliche politische Errungenschaft der Sozial-Ingenieure aus jener Zeit 30, 88. Und es scheint kaum eine Ferienphantasie gegeben zu haben, in die sich nicht eine Spur utopischen Überschusses eingeschrieben hatte. Das neue Recht auf Ferien etwa wuchs zusammen mit dem Traum, sehr schnell an das ferne Ziel jeder Reise zu gelangen. Das erklärt, warum die 1926 gegründete Lufthansa nicht nur mit ihrem im selben Jahr geborenen Kranich warb und mit einem (natürlich bemützten!) Hotelboy, der «Bitte Einsteigen!» ruft 12, sondern auch mit einer, in einer Geste des hochgeschätzten Ausdruckstanzes erstarrten, ideal-schönen Badenden (mit Badekappe!), welche – zwei Faszinationen ihrer Zeit kontaminierend – den potenziellen Kunden rät: «Fliegt in die Bäder!» 11. So wie man mit der Lufthansa schnell «in die Bäder!» kam oder mit der Bal-Air rasch von Lyon über Genf nach Frankfurt 69, konnte man mit dem Ozeanriesen in die Heimat des Tut-Ench Ammon reisen, dessen Mumie 1926 auf Welttournee ging 9 – oder auch unter den Sternenhimmel Südamerikas 74, dessen Rhythmen gerade begannen, der «Neger-» oder «Jazz-Musik» aus Chicago, Saint Louis und New Orleans Konkurrenz zu machen 68.

Buenos Aires, New York, Berlin und Moskau, so habe ich mir einmal vorgestellt, mögen die Hauptstädte des Jahres 1926 gewesen sein. Aber mittlerweile bin ich mir fast sicher, dass *Davos* – das Davos, wo wenig später Ernst Cassirer und Martin Heidegger die Philosophie des 20. Jahrhunderts auf den Weg bringen sollten (so sahen sie es wenigstens selbst), das Davos, wo (eigentlich kaum überraschend) Thomas Manns «Zauberberg» liegen würde – dass Davos die heimliche und eigentliche Hauptstadt von 1926 gewesen ist. Denn Davos war nicht einfach ein weiterer schöner Ferienort – wie zum Beispiel das warme Cattolica an der Adria-Küste 15. Davos war erst durch die kühnen Brückenbauten kühner Ingenieure allgemein erreichbar geworden; Davos lag so hoch und seine Luft war so rein, dass es Hygiene, «Kraft und Gesundheit» versprach 7. Davos war «All the World's Sport Centre» 1 geworden, Weltsportplatz – und das hiess, das Zentrum jener Utopie, in der sich die ehrgeizigen Pläne der Sozial-Ingenieure, die Ansprüche der neuen Sozialpolitik, die Hoffnung auf dauernde Gesundheit und die Träume von der grenzenlosen Verfügung über die Körper trafen. Sport fungierte in der Tat als Schnittpunkt all dieser Ideale und Projektionen, und weil Eislaufen, Skifahren und Tennisspielen vor allem in Davos (oder in St. Moritz) zu einem Mittelklassetraum geworden – aber zugleich ein Oberklassen-privileg geblieben – waren, konnte die Wirklichkeit wohl für einen Moment die Illusion stützen, dass eine Konkretisierung und Sozialisierung dieser kühnsten Versprechun-gen ganz ohne Abstriche an Eleganz möglich seien 19, 22, 27, 28, 78.

Vielleicht – aber das wäre eine Beobachtung, die sich nicht mehr unmittelbar aus den Bildern und Dingen von 1926 ergibt, und ein Zusammenhang, der eher zufällig zu-stande kommt –, vielleicht zeichnete sich in der Mitte der zwanziger Jahre als Mög-lichkeit zum ersten Mal ab, was ich Ihnen bei der Betrachtung der Plakate empfehlen möchte: nämlich ein Verhältnis zu den Dingen der Welt, welches auf die Oberfläche dieser Dinge reagiert und diese Dinge stets ganz zielbewusst benutzt, statt davon besessen zu sein, all den Dingen einen «tieferen Sinn» abzugewinnen. Nicht umsonst gilt die Mitte der zwanziger Jahre ja als einer der grossen Momente in der Geschich-te der *Plakatkunst*; nicht umsonst war 1926 das Jahr, in dem das Bauhaus als eine Ideenschmiede und als Hochschule für angewandte Kunst in Dessau gegründet wurde 4. Denn ein sinnlich-materielles und zugleich betont funktionales Verhältnis zu den Dingen der Welt zu haben, bedeutete gewiss nicht, dass man diesen Dingen einen Sinn, einen Gebrauch, oder eben eine Funktion absprechen wollte. Im Gegenteil: Es gibt kein gutes Plakat ohne implizite Sinn-Zuweisung, welche freilich zugleich zu einer Nutz-Anweisung wird. Aber im Gegensatz zu einer Einstellung gegenüber der Welt, welche sich aus einem unstillbaren Bedürfnis nach «Tiefe» speist, sind die Sinn- und Funktionszuweisungen der Plakate stets prägnant und ohne Überschuss. Das gilt auch und vor allem für jenes Plakat, welches 1926 zum «Künstlerfest der Saison» unter dem Motto «Im Reiche der Reklame» einlud 31. Der Blick des roten Teufels – des Plakatkünstlers – auf das einladende Dekolleté der blonden Dame im schwarzen Abendkleid ist ein auschliesslich aggressiv-erotischer Blick. Nicht mehr als das und eben genau das.
Manchmal drängt sich mir die These auf, dass Martin Heidegger ein ähnlich prägnan-tes, nicht-überschüssiges Verhältnis zu den Dingen der Welt beschreiben wollte, als er 1926 für das Manuskript seines Buches «Sein und Zeit» den Bindestrich-Begriff des «In-der-Welt-seins» erfand. Dieser Begriff des «In-der-Welt-seins» sollte die traditio-nelle Distanz zwischen dem (als rein geistig gedachten) «Subjekt» und den (aus-schliesslich materiell vorgestellten) «Objekten», der Welt der Dinge, minimieren. Leider belegen die aus dem Alltag gegriffenen Beispiele aus Heideggers Buch nicht endgültig, dass «Reklame», wie es damals unter den Fortschrittlichen hiess, eine Inspiration für den Begriff des «In-der-Welt-seins» gewesen war. Aber auf der anderen Seite sind Heideggers Beispiele in «Sein und Zeit» doch auch viel zu unkonventionell, als dass sie eine solche Assoziation ausschlössen. Mit oder ohne Heideggers Rücken-deckung aber – ein Gang durch die Plakate dieses Jahres wird uns zurückbringen in-die-Welt-von-1926.

8 **Michail Čeremnych**
Euch sollen die stachligen Fangarme
abgeklemmt werden
You should have your prickly tentacles
cut off with pincers

9 **Anonym**
Season 1926–27/Cook's
Nile and Palestine Arrangements
Saison 1926–27/Cook's
Nil und Palästina Arrangements

10 **Willy Dzubas**
Deutschland/Berlin
Germany/Berlin

11 **Hans Vogel**
Fliegt in die Bäder!
Deutsche Luft Hansa AG
Fly to the resorts!
Deutsche Luft Hansa AG

12 **Hans Vogel**
Bitte einsteigen!
All aboard!

13 **Trio SA**, Lausanne
Lausanne Ouchy/Plages
Lausanne Ouchy/Beaches

14 **E. Hunter**
Grand Central Terminal/
The Gateway to a Continent/
New York Central Lines
Grand Central Terminal/
Das Tor zu einem Kontinent/
New York Central Lines

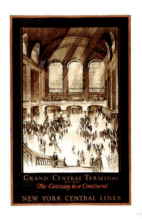

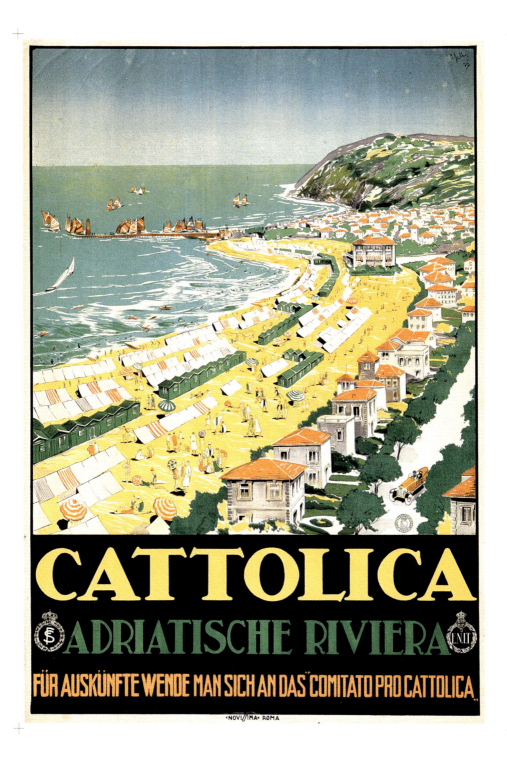

15 **unleserliche Signatur/illegible signature**
Cattolica/Adriatische Riviera
Cattolica/Adriatic Riviera

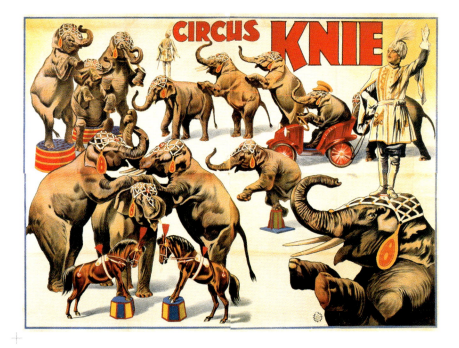

16 **Michail Veksler**
Kinder des Sturms
Children of the Storm

17 **Anonym**
Circus Knie

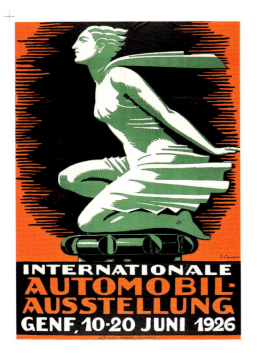

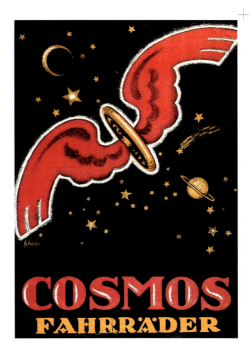

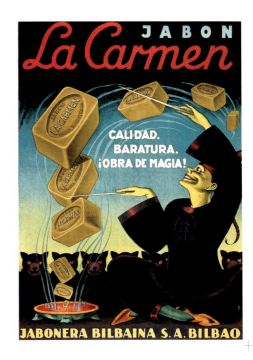

18 **Jules-Ami Courvoisier**
Internationale Automobil-Ausstellung Genf
International Motor Show Geneva

19 **Anonymous**
3. Schweizer. Arbeiterturn- und Sportfest
3rd Swiss Workers' Gymnastic and Sports Festival

20 **Carl Scherer**
Cosmos Fahrräder
Cosmos bicycles

21 **Otto Baumberger**
Seife La Carmen
Carmen soap

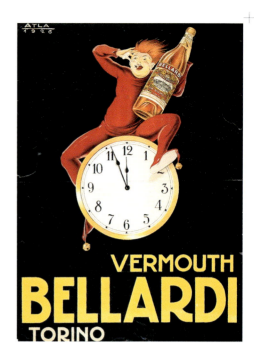

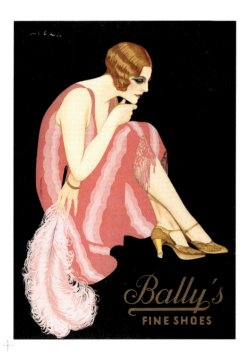

22 **Johann Emil Müller**
Lausanne-Ouchy/Plage
Lausanne-Ouchy/Beach

23 **Ribas**
Bally's Fine Shoes

24 **Atla**
Vermouth Bellardi Torino

25 **Hermann Blaser**
Burger Kehl & Co./PKZ

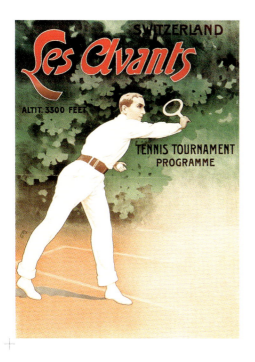

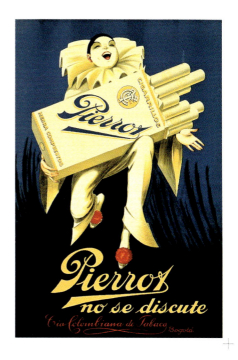

26 **Marcello Nizzoli**
Campari/das feine Aperitif
Campari/the fine apéritif

27 **G.B.**
Les Avants/Tennis Tournament
Les Avants/Tennis Tournier

28 **Anonym**
Mars/das Qualitäts-Rad
Mars/the quality bike

29 **Anonym**
Cigarillos Pierrot/keine Frage
Cigarillos Pierrot/no question

30 **Anonym**
Cigarillos Monte Christo/Poker/Selectos y Rio de Oro/
Mis marcas preferidas
meine Lieblingsmarken
my favourite brands

31 **Lucien Zabel**
Das Künstlerfest der Saison/Im Reiche der Reklame
The artistic festival of the season/in the realm of
the advertisement

32 **Anonym**
Alle zu den Quartier-Wahlen/Wahl des Komitees
für Wohnraumverwaltung
All turn out for the local elections/electing the
housing administration committee

33 **Anonym**
Vergesst uns nicht/Internationale Rote Hilfe
Don't forget us/International Red Aid

34 Anton Lavinskij
Kommunističeskij
internacional/eröffnet das
Abonnement für das Jahr 1926
Kommunističeskij
internacional/take out your
subscription for 1926

35 Robert Stöcklin
Mustermesse Basel 1926/
Meldeschluss 31. Januar
Basel Trade Fair/Closing date for
registration 31 January

36 Ernst Keller
Das Neue Heim/
Kunstgewerbemuseum Zürich
The new home/Zurich Museum
of Arts and Crafts

37 Otto Löbl
Wiener Messe
Vienna Trade Fair

38 Franz von Stuck
1. Allgemeine Kunstausstellung
München/Neue Secession
1st General Munich Art Exhibition/
New Secession

39 Otto Baumberger
Löwenbräu Zürich

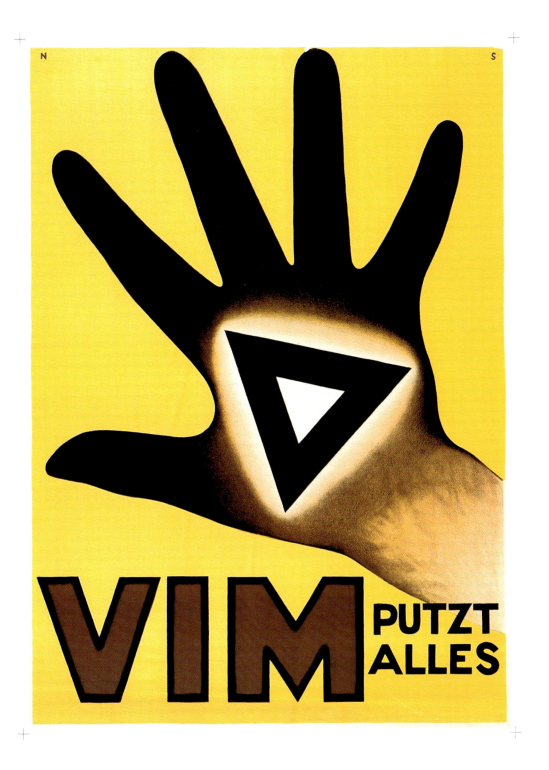

40 **Niklaus Stoecklin**
Vim putzt alles
Vim cleans everything

41 **Karl Bickel**
So kleidet PKZ
This is how PKZ clothes look

42 **Edward Mc Knight Kauffer**
The Indian Museum/Book To South Kensington

43 **Jacqueline Marval**
Une nuit à Chang-hai
Eine Nacht in Shanghai
A Night in Shanghai

44 **J. van den Bergh**
Chemins de fer de l'Etat Belge/Les Ardennes Belges
Belgische Staatsbahnen/Die belgischen Ardennen
Belgian State Railways/The Belgian Ardennes

45 **Hugo Laubi**
Arosa

46 **Carl Moos**
Löw Schuhe
Löw shoes

47 **Otto Baumberger**
Firn Ice Cream

A YEAR AS PART OF YOUR SURROUNDINGS

Hans Ulrich Gumbrecht

Every day in the months it took to write the book "In 1926. Living at the Edge of Time" I dreamed that this year might become part of my surroundings. To put it more precisely: the ideal that I wanted to approach with my text, without quite naïvely overlooking the effective boundaries placed on "text" as a medium, was the notion of the year 1926 as a room that I would be able to walk about in. At first this was nothing more than a more concrete and intense version of the old metaphor of "immersing oneself" in a past world. And "immersing myself" like this has always been so much one of my favourite occupations that I am now convinced that being fascinated with "immersing oneself" is common ground for all the different versions of the many–academic and non-academic–forms of historical culture. Learning from history and the philosophy of history, archaeology and collecting antiques, historical novels and history painting, all these practices, in my opinion, require the primary fascination of "immersing oneself" in the past, and they draw inspiration and energy from that past.

At first I didn't even for a second think about making my dream come true, or even believe that it might, but now it has indeed come true in the Museum für Gestaltung's poster exhibition–and because this exhibition makes it possible to walk through memories of the year 1926 that have become our surroundings, a room, this has–paradoxically–yielded the maximum of everything that I would never have dared to hope for in a book about 1926. I mean this–despite the paradoxical formulation–in a very precise sense, and not least in a negative sense: it would be to misunderstand my book–and this exhibition as well–if one tried to wrest something like a "more profound understanding" of the year 1926 from them. Wanting to understand the year more profoundly, or even to understand it better, would on the one hand mean associating it with the previous events and movements that might have produced *The Year 1926;* and on the other hand it would also mean bringing the year into line with all the subsequent developments for which we could see it as a "historical turning-point". And so intending *to understand a year,* surprisingly perhaps, means that one does *not concentrate primarily on the year itself;* and a perspective like this that goes beyond the year in question then inevitably brings with it the duty to select a "significant year", a "threshold year" for historical work, a year that should help to explain as much as possible about what came before it and as much as possible about what came after it. Certainly understanding things like this is still important and anyway legitimate–but it was never part of the dream that I associated with my book and that is now coming true in this exhibition. What I wanted to do was to let *just the surfaces of the year 1926,* its sounds, feelings and smells, its shapes, colours and outlines, *work on my senses*–and this was not because I might have ascribed any particular significance to this year. My entire motivation–academically an extremely problematical one–was that I had thought for so long that two of my grandparents had died in 1926 that I had developed something like a specific 1926-related craving. Anyone who immerses himself in a room, a set of surroundings, made up of the past like this will discover that many shapes and themes in these surroundings soon repeat themselves – and repeat themselves in a surprising way. Quite a number of the things that one registers on a first, second and third glance not only keep returning, but return in ever-new contexts and recombinations, and it is not possible to reduce their sequence to a formula. And it is precisely these, these unpredictable but incessant recurrences, that create the identity of a period of time in which one is immersing oneself (without actually wanting to understand it). Twenty or more years ago, when semiotics was peaking on the theory exchange in the directors' suites occupied by arts academics and culture managers, one would probably have tried to systematize an impression and a set of findings like this by an attempt at writing a "grammar" of the appropriate cultural and historical moment. At that time the culture academics and culture professionals would have been determined to outdo the exhibition visitors' superficial impression with a "deeper insight". Today we are a little more relaxed, I hope. Just like the exhibition visitors (the only difference being that that we are able to take our time over it and as a rule we are even paid for it), we cultural historians pursue such recurrent forms and themes within a historical period patiently and with growing fascination – as an unpredictable sequence, that cannot be reduced to a formula but constantly gains in density and intensity. We pursue it as what the French philosophers Gilles Deleuze and Félix Guattari once called a "rhizome": a tissue of affinities and associations that is neither infinite nor sharply defined, neither unbroken nor discontinuous.

Perhaps when you take your very first look at the posters (this happened to me a few years ago), you will discover that 1926 was to an extent *obsessed with headgear.* But of course at the time no one saw this as something special, or as a universal symptom. Why does the little boy in the foreground of the poster for the film Buster's Mix-Up 3 have a sailor's hat that sticks out so much at the top, and what is growing out of the head of the girl on his right? A proto-form of Mickey Mouse ears, perhaps? It would be better for you to get used as soon as possible to the fact that there is scarcely ever an answer to 'why' questions like this. If you want to earn your right to explore the posters in the show, would do better to make free associations between your observations, so that you can establish a series of structural affinities by observing freely like this. Then you will probably notice that the pot-bellied creature representing the state in the appeal against the public "housing construction initiative" in 1926 64 is wearing a mercenary foot-soldier's cap with an enormous feather in it, and that scarcely any of the figures inspired by Greek antiquity that you will frequently come across ever show their hair. They have put on the helmet of Hermes the messenger god with its little wings, or ancient soldiers' helmets with half-visors, the chosen headgear of Pallas Athene, with many emblems of wisdom 38 – or even, quite anachronistically, the Phrygian Cap that has adorned the head of Marianne, France's allegorical figure since the revolution in the late eighteenth century. And if there actually is some hair to be seen it is extremely stylized; most usually in a bob, that close-cropped boy's hair-do, always shown as black, that emphasizes the geometrical cut of the clothes in which female forms are so easily concealed. But even images from the otherwise frugal Soviet Union can go to the other extreme: turbans braided into the woman's hair, spilling out into stands and then appearing to explode the space around the head in question 76 like the locks of the terrifying Medusa (or the feelers of an outsize insect).

So let yourself and your imagination be infected by a past exploratory joy, joy triggered by the experiment, which probably seemed to have absolutely no limits in 1926, of varying and changing "natural" forms and positions for the human body "artificially" and in every direction imaginable. Women at the height of fashion want to look like adolescent men, and men had never used as much make-up as they did in the twenties since the 17th century (have you ever noticed that even Thomas Mann wore *rouge*?). Draping bodies with live ornaments was an aesthetic passion in the variety shows and circuses of that world 1, 17, 19, 55. This kind of pleasure in experimenting with changing things that looked natural until shortly before definitely developed into a political style as well. This was the time when educationalists and reforming politicians liked to call themselves "social engineers". It was not just the intellectuals of 1926 who were fascinated by the Soviet Union as an apparently limitless planning project of this kind 8, 75. Never, I fear, were social hierarchies seen less as an immutable fate than then: no strike seemed to have impossible aims, and no statistics, no self-presentation, no travel report from the former Russian workers' and peasants' paradise sounded too optimistic to be taken seriously 32, 80. A trivial version of the symmetrical dreams of the new society was the furore about hygiene that had just overcome the European Middle Classes 77. Bobbed hair, Charleston dress and a little domestic ambition to have the most shiny-clean pumice stone were by no means incompatible.

In case you are not familiar with it as a historical fact, you can experience it *live* and almost uncut with the posters in the exhibition: the general strike triggered by the English miners in 1926 did fail 5 and we have now long since dismissed the Soviet Union as the most catastrophic failed experiment in human history, but we still have the twenties to thank for the fact that *holidays* are generally expected and seen as an inalienable right. Exuberant Italian beaches 15, the romantic Ardennes in Belgium 44 and the majestic Swiss Alps 45–47 were suddenly no longer just motifs for painter, something for geographers to describe and a challenge for a very few sportsmen. In the contemporary imagination they had all become places of rest, relaxation and recreation, spaces that opened up to the bodies of people who had worked hard and almost uninterruptedly. Though if true politics actually was the "art of the possible", then holidays–rather than the radical utopias of the completely new society–were the actual political achievement of the social engineers of the day 30, 88. And there seems to have been scarcely a holiday fantasy that did not carry a trace of utopian excess. For instance, the new right to holidays grew with the dream of getting to the distant destination involved in any journey very rapidly. This explains why Lufthansa, which was founded in 1926, not only used their crane, born in the same year, in their advertisements, along with a hotel boy (in a cap, of course!), shouting "All aboard!"12, but also a female bather of idealized beauty (in a bathing-cap!), frozen into a pose from the highly-esteemed world of interpretative dancing, and advising the potential customer – thus conflating two fascinations of her day – to "Fly to the resorts!" 11. Just as you reached "the resorts" quickly with Lufthansa, or got to Frankfurt from Lyon via Geneva with Bal-Air 69, you could sail on a giant ocean-going liner to the home of Tutankhamun, whose mummy went on a world tour in 1926 9 – or also find yourself under the starry skies of South America 74, whose rhythms were just start-ing to compete with the "Negro" or "jazz" music from Chicago, Saint Louis and New Orleans 68.

I once imagined that Buenos Aires, New York, Berlin and Moscow might have been the capitals of 1926. But in the mean time I am almost sure that *Davos* – the Davos where Ernst Cassirer and Martin Heidegger were later to set 20th century philosophy on its way (at least that's how they saw it), the Davos where (actually hardly surprisingly) Thomas Mann's "Magic Mountain" would be set – that Davos was the secret and actual capital of 1926. For Davos was not just simply another beautiful holiday resort – like for example warm Cattolica on the Adriatic coast 15. Davos had only become generally accessible because of the bold bridges built by bold engineers; Davos was so high and its air was so pure that it promised hygiene, "strength and health" 7. Davos was "All the World's Sport Centre" 1 – and that meant the centre of the utopia in which the ambitious plans of the social engineers, the aims of the new social policy, hopes of lasting health and dreams of limitlessly available bodies came togeth-er. In fact sport functioned as the interface for all these ideals and projections, and because ice-skating, skiing and tennis had become a middle-class dream above all in Davos (or in St. Moritz) – but at the same time remained an upper-class privilege – reality could perhaps for a moment support the illusion that concretization and socialization of these boldest of promises were possible without conceding anything in terms of elegance 19, 22, 27, 28, 78.

Perhaps – but that would be an observation that does not emerge directly from the images and things of 1926, and a connection that may be a little more random –, perhaps in the mid twenties a possibility was emerging for the first time that I would like to commend to your attention while you are looking at the posters: and that is a relationship of things to the world that responds to the surface of these things, and always uses these things with a definite purpose, rather than being obsessed with wresting a "more profound meaning" from everything. There is a good reason for seeing the mid twenties as one of the great moments in the history of poster art; there is good reason for the fact that 1926 was the year in which the Bauhaus was established in Dessau as a smithy for ideas and school of applied art 4. Because having a sensually material and at the same time emphatically functional relationship with the world certainly does not mean that one wants to deny these things a sense, a use, or even a function. On the contrary: there is no good poster without an implicit allocation of meaning, though admittedly this becomes an allocation of use at the same time. But in contrast with an attitude to the world that feeds on an insatiable need for "depth", the posters' allocations of sense and function are always succinct and without excess. This also and above all applies to the poster that in 1926 issued its invitation to the "artistic festival of the season" with the motto "in the realm of the advertisement" 31. The way the red devil – the poster artist – is looking at the décolleté of the blond woman in the black evening dress is exclusively aggressive and erotic. No more than that, but precisely that.

I sometimes feel compelled to entertain the idea that Martin Heidegger was trying to describe a similarly succinct, non-excessive relationship with the things of the world when he invented the hyphenated concept of "being-in-the-world" for the manuscript of his book "Sein und Zeit" in 1926. This notion of "being-in-the-world" was intended to minimize the traditional distance between the "subject" (imagined purely intellectually) and the "objects" (seen exclusively materially), the world of things. Unfortunately the everyday examples that Heidegger uses in his book do not ultimately support the idea that "Reklame" (advertising), as progressive people called it, had inspired the concept of "being-in-the-world". But on the other hand Heidegger's examples in "Sein und Zeit" are perhaps too unconventional to exclude an association of this kind. But with or without Heidegger's backing – a walk through the posters from this year will put us back in-the-world-of-1926.

48 **Anton Lavinskij**
Die Solotänzerin ihrer Hoheit
Her Highness's Solo Dancer

49 **Ludwig Hohlwein**
Frühling in Wiesbaden
Spring in Wiesbaden

50 **Jäck**
Hendes Spanier

51 **MS**
Maskenbälle Waldhaus Dolder Zürich
Masked Balls Waldhaus Dolder Zurich

52 **Hugo Siegwart**
Eidgenössisches Schwing- u. Älplerfest Luzern
Swiss wrestling and Alpine farming festival, Lucerne

53 Otto Baumberger
Kunsthaus Maskenfest Baur au Lac Zürich

54 Ludwig Hohlwein
Use Star Herb
Verwenden Sie Star Herb

55 André B.
Teddy-Ted and Partner

56 Anonym
Gracias! Siempre fumo Virginia!
Danke! Ich rauche Virginia!
Thank you! Mine's a Virginia!

57 **Nikolaj Prusakov**
Gesetz und Pflicht (Amok)
Law and Duty (Amok)

58 **Nikolaj Prusakov/Gregorij Borisov**
Die Erste und die Letzte
The First and the Last

59 **Jakov Ruklevskij**
Café Fanconi

60 **Jakov Ruklevskij/Vladimir Stenberg**
Nach dem Gesetz
According to the Law

61 **Anton Lavinskij**
Der Verräter
The Traitor

62 Otto Plattner
Extrazulage an Arbeitslose/Nein
Extra unemployment benefit/No

63 Otto Plattner
Zwangs-Arbeitslosen-Versicherung/Nein
Compulsory unemployment insurance/No

64 Otto Plattner
Wohnungsbau-Initiative/Nein!
Housing construction initiative/No!

65 Hans Beatus Wieland
Herunter mit dem Brotkorb! Brotmonopol Nein!
Lower the bread-basket! Bread monopoly No!

MITTELSTAND STIMM

GEWERBE, HANDEL
JNDUSTRIE, FREIE
BERUFE, ANGE-
STELLTE, BE-
AMTE STIMMT
FREISINNIG. UNSERE
ZIELE: 1. SPARSAME STAATS-
UND GEMEINDEVERWAL-
TUNG. 2. WENIGER BELAS-
TUNG UND WENIGER BE-
LÄSTIGUNG IN STEUER-
SACHEN. 3. RASCHE HILFE
FÜR ÜBERLASTETE GE-
MEINDEN. 4. ZWECK-
MÄSSIGE FÖRDER-
UNG DES WOH-
NUNGSBAU-
ES/FREI-
SIN-
NIGE
PARTEI DES KAN-
TONS ZUERICH

FREISINNIG

WOLFSBERG ZÜRICH
985.

Käch

66 **Walter Käch**
Mittelstand/stimm freisinnig
Middle classes/vote Liberal

45

67 **Charles Gesmar**
Casino de Paris / Rougemont / Mistinguett

68 **Anonym**
1. Internat. Tanzturnier im Baur au Lac Zürich
1st International Dancing Tournament in Baur
au Lac Zürich

69 **Niklaus Stoecklin**
Balair Line/Frankfurt/Karlsruhe/Basel/Genève/Lyon

70 **Anonym**
11.093 Gewinne/Preis des Loses 50 Kopeken
11,093 prizes/ticket price 50 kopeks

71 **Fritz Rosen**
Nach Berlin! Jeder einmal in Berlin
Berlin here we come! Everyone must see Berlin once

72 **Fougasse**
Too much waiting, too little room/Plenty of room
and no waiting/London Underground

73 **Jacob Jongert**
Holland/Utrecht

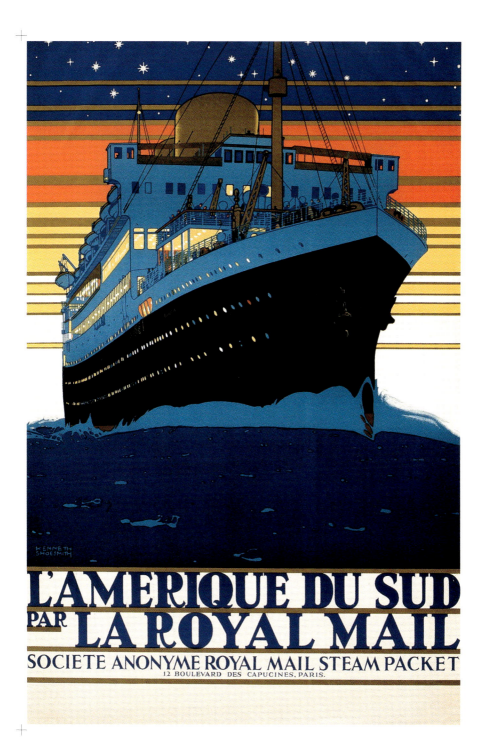

74 **Kenneth Shoesmith**
L'Amérique du Sud par la Royal Mail
Süd-Amerika mit Royal Mail
South America by Royal Mail

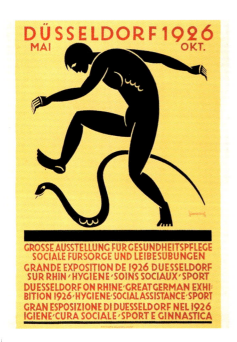

75 **Iosif Gerasimovič**
Salamandra

76 **Richard Schwarzkopf**
Düsseldorf 1926/Grosse Ausstellung für Gesundheits-
pflege sociale Fürsorge und Leibesübungen
Great exhibition/Hygiene Social Assistance Sport

77 **Nikolaj Kogout**
Der Kaiser der Herrschenden und der Gott der
Herrschenden
The Emperor of the Rulers and the God of the Rulers

78 **Anonym**
Grand Tournoi International St. Moritz

79 **Eric de Coulon**
Blanc/au bon marché
Weisswaren/au bon marché
Whites/au bon marché

80 **Anonym**
Die Arbeit des 7. Kongresses der Gewerkschaften der
UdSSR, Dezember 1926/Unsere Losung: näher zu
den Massen
The work of the 7th USSR Trade Unions' Congress,
December 1926/Our solution: closer to the masses

81 **Ernst Böhm**
Grosse Polizeiausstellung Berlin 1926
Grand Police Exhibition Berlin 1926

82 **Otto Baumberger**
Ausverkauf Teppichhaus Forster & Co
Carpet sale by Forster & Co

83 **Helmuth Kurtz**
Völkerkundliche Ausstellung der Basler Mission
Basel Mission Ethnological Exhibition

84 **Hubert Saget**
Forta/das unverwüstliche Haarband
Forta/the indestructible hair-ribbon

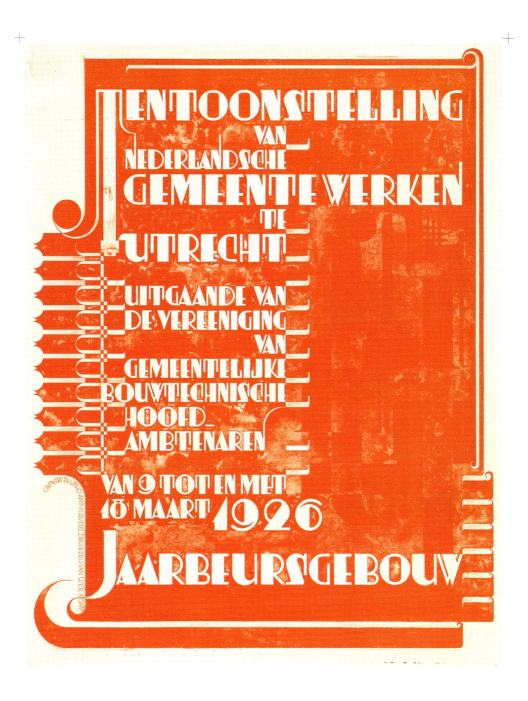

85 **Antoon Kurvers**
Tentoonstelling van Nederlandsche Gemeente Werken
te Utrecht
Exhibition of Dutch Municipal Works in Utrecht

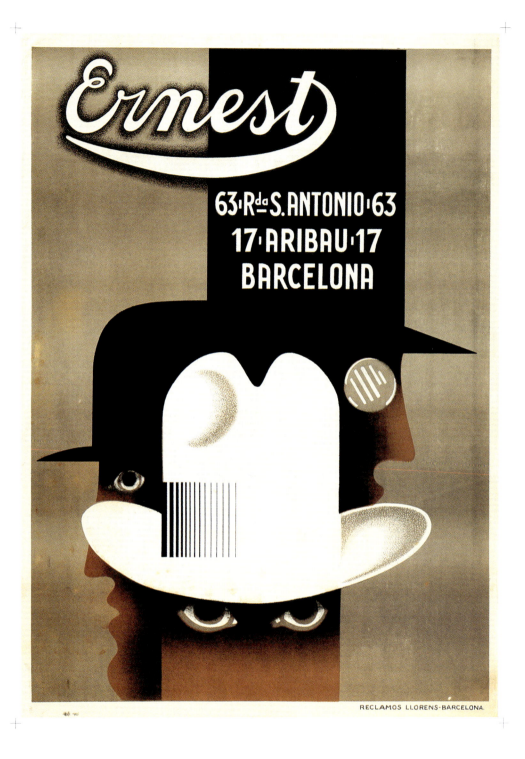

86 **Cassandre**
Ernest/Barcelona

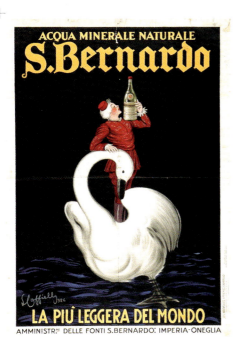

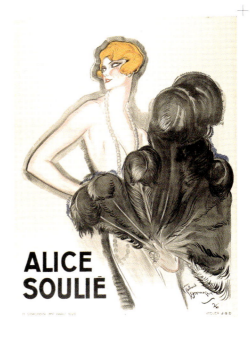

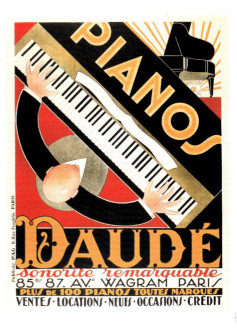

87 Leonetto Cappiello
Mineralwasser San Bernardo/das leichteste der Welt
San Bernardo mineral water/the lightest in the world

88 Eric de Coulon
Neuchâtel Plage
Neuchâtel Beach

89 Jean-Gabriel Domergue
Alice Soulié

90 André Daudé
Pianos Daudé/sonorité remarquable
Daudé Klaviere/ausserordentliche Klangfülle
Daudé pianos/remarkable sonority

91 **Emil Cardinaux**
Bally Schuhe
Bally shoes

Katalog

Alle abgebildeten Plakate stammen, mit Ausnahme der Nr. 5, aus der Plakatsammlung des Museums für Gestaltung Zürich und wurden für die Publikation neu bearbeitet.

Die Daten des Katalogs folgen den Rubriken Gestaltung, Lebensdaten, Plakattext, Erscheinungsjahr, Erscheinungsland, Drucktechnik, Format. Dabei gelten folgende Regelungen:

Gestaltung: es werden der vollständige Name und die Lebensdaten angegeben.

Plakattext: Die beste Wiedergabe des Texts bietet die Abbildung des Plakates selbst. Darum wird hier eine vereinfachte Form wiedergegeben, welche nur die aussagekräftigsten Textbestandteile berücksichtigt. Allfällige Umstellungen dienen der Verständlichkeit. Das Zeichen / trennt inhaltliche Texteinheiten.

Erscheinungsjahr: Wenn nicht anders vermerkt, stammen die Plakate aus dem Jahr 1926. Unscharfe Datierungen stellten in dieser Publikation vor ein besonderes Dilemma: wäre «ca. 1925» nicht auch «ca. 1926»? Wir entschieden uns, ohne Kosmetik auszukommen und in Zweifelsfällen den Jahresangaben des Bestandeskatalogs zu folgen. Plakate, die bisher undatiert waren und aus stilistischen oder inhaltlichen Gründen in den Zeitraum um 1926 passen, werden mit «Mitte der zwanziger Jahre» gekennzeichnet.

Erscheinungsland: Das Land wird mit dem international gebräuchlichen Code angegeben; wenn es abweicht von der Nationalität bzw. dem hauptsächlichen Tätigkeitsland des Gestalters, so wird der Ländercode auch seinem Namen beigegeben.

Drucktechnik: Die englische Übersetzung der Drucktechnik erschliesst sich meist aus dem deutschen Begriff wie Lithografie oder Offset. Buchdruck wird übersetzt mit letterpress; Linoldruck mit lino print.

Format: die Angaben werden in der Abfolge Höhe × Breite und in cm gemacht. Weil die Plakate oft nicht exakt rechtwinklig geschnitten sind, werden die Abmessungen auf halbe cm aufgerundet.

Bei den mit * markierten Plakaten hat sich erst nach der definitiven Bildauswahl ergeben, dass es sich um Nachdrucke handelt.

Die Plakatgeschichte ist ein junges Forschungsgebiet – verlässliche Informationen sind rar. Alle Unsicherheiten werden mit [?] markiert und signalisieren, dass jeder Hinweis und jede Ergänzung willkommen ist: plakat.sammlung@museum-gestaltung.ch.

Catalogue

All the posters illustrated with the exception of no. 5 are from the Museum für Gestaltung Zürich's poster collection and were specially prepared for publication.

The data in the catalogue are under the headings design, dates of birth and death, poster text, year of appearance, country of first appearance, printing technique, format. The following rules have been applied:

Design: the full name and dates of birth and death are given.

Poster text: the poster itself provides the best version of the text. Thus a simplified form is used here, giving only the most meaningful elements of the text. Any rearrangements that have been made are for purposes of intelligibility. The sign / separates textual units by content.

Year of appearance: if not noted otherwise, all posters date from the year 1926. Approximate dating presents a particular dilemma in this publication: is "c. 1925" not very much the same as "c. 1926"? We decided to avoid cosmetic solutions and to follow the years given in the museum's collection catalogue in case of doubt. Posters that were previously undated and fit into the period around 1926 for reasons of style or content are dated "Mitte der zwanziger Jahre" ("mid twenties").

Country of first appearance: the country is indicated with the customary international code letter(s); if this designation differs from the designer's nationality or usual country of work then the country code is appended to the designer's name.

Printing technique: the English translation of the printing technique is usually suggested by the German concept, as in Lithografie or Offset. Buchdruck is translated by letterpress; Linoldruck by lino print.

Format: the details are given in the sequence height × width and in cm. Because the posters are often not cut exactly at right angles, the dimensions are rounded off to half cm.

In the case of the posters marked with * we did not establish that they were reprints until after the final selection of images for the book.

The history of posters is a recent field of research – reliable information is rare. Any uncertainties are marked with [?], which signals that any references or additional material are welcome: plakat.sammlung@museum-gestaltung.ch

1 Carl Franz Moos (1878−1959)
Davos / All the World's
Sport Centre
CH Lithografie 90 × 64

2 Anonym
6000 politische Gefangene / Das
ist das Polen Pilsudskis / Erzwingt
die Amnestie! − 6000 political
prisoners / This is Pilsudski's
Poland / Force an amnesty!
ca. 1925
DE Lithografie 72 × 48,5

3 Anonym
Stern Brothers present Buster's
Mix-up
US Lithografie 104 × 68

4 Herbert Bayer (1900−1985)
Kandinsky Jubiläums-Ausstellung
zum 60. Geburtstag − Kandinsky's
60th birthday anniversary
exhibition
DE Buchdruck 48,5 × 62
Basler Plakatsammlung

5 Anonym
Down with the sweaters!
A general strike! − Nieder mit den
Ausbeutern! Generalstreik!
GB Buchdruck 36 × 50

6 Marcello Nizzoli (1887−1969)
F N (Fabrique Nationale)
ca. 1925
IT Lithografie 119 × 79,5

7 Otto Morach (1887−1973)
Der Weg zur Kraft u. Gesundheit
führt über Davos − The way to
strength and health is via Davos
CH Lithografie 128 × 90,5

8 Michail Michajlov Čeremnych
(1890−1962)
Euch sollen die stachligen
Fangarme abgeklemmt werden
− You should have your prickly
tentacles cut off with pincers
ca. 1925
SU Lithografie 38 × 26,5

9 Anonym
Season 1926−27 / Cook's Nile and
Palestine Arrangements − Saison
1926−27 / Cook's Nil und Palästina
Arrangements
GB Offset, Buchdruck 100 × 62,5

10 Willy Dzubas (1877−1947)
Deutschland / Berlin − Germany /
Berlin
DE Offset 101 × 63

11 Hans Vogel
Fliegt in die Bäder! Deutsche Luft
Hansa AG − Fly to the resorts!
ca. 1926
DE Offset* 67 × 47

12 Hans Vogel
Bitte einsteigen! − All aboard!
ca. 1926
DE Offset* 64,5 × 43,5

13 Trio SA, Lausanne
Lausanne-Ouchy / Plages −
Strandbad − Beaches
CH Lithografie 100 × 64

14 E. Hunter
Grand Central Terminal / The
Gateway to a Continent / New York
Central Lines − Das Tor zu einem
Kontinent
US Lithografie 104 × 69

15 unlesbare Signatur / illegible
signature
Cattolica / Adriatische Riviera −
Adriatic Riviera
IT Lithografie 100 × 69,5

16 Michail Veksler (1898−?)
Kinder des Sturms − Children
of the Storm / Regie: Fr. Ermler,
E. Loganson, Kamera:
N. Aptekman, Ausstattung:
E. Enej, Prod.: Leningradkino
SU Lithografie 70 × 106

17 Anonym
Circus Knie
DE Lithografie 135 × 183

18 Jules-Ami Courvoisier
(1884−1936)
Internationale Automobil-
Ausstellung Genf − International
Motor Show Geneva
CH Lithografie 127 × 90

19 Anonym
3. Schweizer. Arbeiterturn- und
Sportfest Bern − 3rd Swiss
Worker's Gymnastic and Sports
Festival
CH Lithografie 127,5 × 90,5

20 Carl Scherer (1890−1953)
Cosmos Fahrräder − bicycles
CH Lithografie 127 × 90

21 Otto Baumberger
(1889−1961, CH)
Jabon La Carmen − Seife
La Carmen − La Carmen Soap
ca. 1925
ES Lithografie 100 × 70

22 Johann Emil Müller
(1885−1958)
Lausanne-Ouchy / Plage − Strandbad − Beach
CH Lithografie 127 × 90

23 Ribas (ES)
Bally's Fine Shoes
CH Lithografie 127 × 90

24 Atla
Vermouth Bellardi Torino
IT Lithografie 128 × 89

25 Hermann Blaser
Burger Kehl & Co. / PKZ
CH Lithografie 127 × 90

26 Marcello Nizzoli (1887−1969)
Campari / das feine Aperitif − the
fine apéritif
IT Lithografie 128 × 89,5

27 G.B.
Les Avants / Tennis Tournament −
Tennis Tournier
ca. 1925
CH Lithografie 107 × 76,5

28 Anonym
Mars / das Qualitäts-Rad −
the quality bike
1925
DE Lithografie 57,5 × 39,5

29 Anonym
Cigarillos Pierrot / no se discute −
keine Frage − no question
ca. 1925
CH Lithografie 60 × 42

30 Anonym
Cigarillos / Monte Christo / Poker /
Selectos y Rio de Oro / Mis marcas
preferidas − meine Lieblingsmarken − my favourite brands
ca. 1925
CH Lithografie 42 × 60

31 Lucien Zabel (1893−1936)
Das Künstlerfest der Saison / Im
Reiche der Reklame − The artistic
festival of the season / in the realm
of the advertisement
DE Lithografie 72 × 96

32 Anonym
Alle zu den Quartier-Wahlen / Wahl
des Komitees für Wohnraumverwaltung − All turn out for the
local elections / electing the
housing administration committee
ca. 1926
SU Lithografie 38 × 56,5

33 Anonym
Vergesst uns nicht/Internationale
Rote Hilfe – Don't forget us/
International Red Aid
ca. 1925
SY Lithografie 59 × 79

34 Anton Michajlovič Lavinskij
(1893–1968)
Kommunisticeskij
internacional/eröffnet das Abonnement für das Jahr 1926 – take
out your subscription for 1926
SU Lithografie 72 × 54

35 Robert Stöcklin (1889–1931)
Mustermesse Basel 1926/Melde-
schluss 31. Januar – Basel Trade
Fair/Closing date for registration
31 january
CH Lithografie 127 × 90

36 Ernst Keller (1891–1968)
Das Neue Heim/Kunstgewerbe-
museum Zürich – The new home
/Zurich Museum of Arts and
Crafts
CH Lithografie 127 × 90

37 Otto Löbl (tätig ca. 1926–1938)
Wiener Messe – Vienna Trade Fair
AT Lithografie 123 × 93

38 Franz von Stuck (1863–1928)
1. Allgemeine Kunstausstellung
München/Neue Secession –
1st General Munich Art Exhibition/
New Secession
DE Lithografie 124,5 × 88

39 Otto Baumberger (1889–1961)
Löwenbräu Zürich
CH Lithografie 128 × 90,5

40 Niklaus Stoecklin (1896–1982)
Vim putzt alles – VIM cleans
everything
CH Lithografie 127 × 90

41 Karl Bickel (1886–1982)
So kleidet PKZ – This is how PKZ
clothes look
CH Lithografie 127 × 90

42 Jacqueline Marval
(1866–1932)
Une nuit à Chang-hai
– Eine Nacht in Shanghai
– A Night in Shanghai
Mitte der zwanziger Jahre
FR Lithografie 119 × 70

43 Edward Leland Mc Knight
Kauffer (1890–1954)
The Indian Museum – Book
To South Kensington
Mitte der zwanziger Jahre
GB Lithografie 102 × 63

44 J. van den Bergh
Chemins de fer de l'Etat Belge/
Les Ardennes Belges – Belgische
Staatsbahnen/Die belgischen
Ardennen – Belgian State
Railways/The Belgian Ardennes
BE Lithografie 104 × 70,5

45 Hugo Laubi (1888–1959)
Arosa
CH Lithografie 127 × 90

46 Carl Franz Moos (1878–1959)
Löw Schuhe – Löw shoes
CH Lithografie 127 × 90

47 Otto Baumberger (1889–1961)
Firn Ice Cream
CH Lithografie 128 × 90,5

48 Anton Michajlovič Lavinskij
(1893–1968)
Die Solotänzerin ihrer Hoheit
– Her Highness's Solo Dancer/
Regie: M. Verner, Kamera:
A. Lemberg
SU Lithografie 137 × 104

49 Ludwig Hohlwein (1874–1949)
Frühling in Wiesbaden – Spring
in Wiesbaden
vermutlich 1927
DE Lithografie 86 × 60

50 Jäck
Hendes Spanier
DK Lithografie 95 × 64

51 MS
Maskenbälle Waldhaus Dolder
Zürich – Masked Balls Waldhaus
Dolder Zürich
CH Lithografie 127 × 90

52 Hugo Siegwart (1865–1938)
Eidgenössisches Schwing-
u. Älplerfest Luzern – Swiss
wrestling and Alpine farming
festival Lucerne
CH Lithografie 127 × 90

53 Otto Baumberger (1889–1961)
Kunsthaus Maskenfest Baur au
Lac Zürich – Masked Balls
CH Lithografie 127 × 90

54 Ludwig Hohlwein
(1874–1949, DE)
Use Star Herb/Medicines and
Teas/for all Diseases/Made from
Imported German Herbs –
Verwenden Sie Star Herb/Medizin
und Tee gegen jede Krankheit/
Hergestellt aus importierten
deutschen Kräutern
ca. 1925
US Lithografie 68 × 40,5

55 André B.
Teddy-Ted and Partner
FR Lithografie 120 × 80,5

56 Anonym
Gracias! Siempre fumo Virginia! –
Danke! Ich rauche Virginia! –
Thank you! Mine's a Virginia!
Mitte der zwanziger Jahre
CH Lithografie 99,5 × 70

57 Nikolaj Prusakov (1900–1952)
/Gregorij Borisov (1899–?)
Gesetz und Pflicht (Amok) – Law
and Duty/Regie: K. Mardčanov,
Kamera: S. Zablosaev
SU Lithografie 104 × 69

58 Nikolaj Prusakov (1900–1952)
/Gregorij Borisov (1899–?)
Die Erste und die Letzte – The
First and the Last/Regie:
Č. Berečvili, Kamera: A. Polikevič
SU Lithografie 104 × 69

59 Jakov Ruklevskij (1884–1965)
Café Fanconi/Regie: M.
Kapčinskij, Kamera: Levickij
SU Lithografie 107 × 72

60 Jakov Ruklevskij (1884–1965)
/Vladimir Stenberg (1899–1982)
Nach dem Gesetz – According
to the Law/Regie: L. Kulečov,
Kamera: K. Kuznecov,
Hauptdarsteller: A. Chochlova,
S. Komarov, V. Fogel'
SU Lithografie 99 × 71

61 Anton Michajlovič Lavinskij
(1893–1968)
Der Verräter – The Traitor/Regie:
A. Room, Kamera: E. Slavinskij
SU Lithografie 108 × 71

62 Otto Plattner (1886–1951)
Extrazulage an Arbeitslose/Nein –
Extra unemployment benefit/No
CH Lithografie 127 × 90

63 Otto Plattner (1886–1951)
Zwangs-Arbeitslosen-Versiche-
rung/Nein – Compulsory
unemployment insurance/No
CH Lithografie 127 × 90

64 Otto Plattner (1886–1951)
Wohnungsbau-Initiative/Nein! –
Housing construction initiative/No!
CH Lithografie 127 × 90

65 Hans Beatus Wieland
(1867–1945)
Herunter mit dem Brotkorb!
/Brotmonopol Nein! – Lower
the bread-basket!/Bread
monopoly No!
CH Lithografie 128 × 90,5

66 Walter Käch (1901–1970)
Mittelstand stimm freisinnig –
Middle classes/vote Liberal
CH Lithografie 127 × 90

67 Charles Gesmar (1900–1928)
Casino de Paris/Rougemont/
Mistinguett
ca. 1926
FR Lithografie 120 × 80

68 Anonym
1. Internat. Tanzturnier im Baur
au Lac Zürich – 1st International
Dancing Tournament in Baur au
Lac Zürich
CH Lithografie 127 × 90

69 Niklaus Stoecklin (1896–1982)
Balair Line/Frankfurt Karlsruhe
Basel Genève Lyon
CH Lithografie 128 × 90

70 Anonym
11.093 Gewinne/Preis des Loses
50 Kopeken – 11,093 prizes/
ticket price 50 kopeks
SU Lithografie 90 × 69

71 Fritz Rosen (1890–1980)
Nach Berlin!/Jeder einmal
in Berlin – Berlin here we come!/
Everyone must see Berlin once
DE Offset 82,5 × 59,5

72 Fougasse [Cyril Kenneth Bird]
(1887–1965)
Too much waiting, too little room/
Plenty of room and no waiting/
London Underground – Zu lange
Wartezeiten, kein Platz/Viel
Platz und keine Wartezeiten/
London Underground
ca. 1925
GB Lithografie 102 × 61

73 Jacob Jongert (1883–1942)
Holland/Utrecht
1926
NL Lithografie 118 × 80

74 Kenneth D. Shoesmith
(1890–1939)
L'Amérique du Sud par la
Royal Mail – Süd-Amerika mit
Royal Mail – South America
by Royal Mail
ca. 1925
GB Lithografie 101 × 63

75 Nikolaj Kogout (1891–1959)
Der Kaiser der Herrschenden
und der Gott der Herrschenden –
The Emperor of the Rulers and
the God of the Rulers
Mitte der zwanziger Jahre
SU Lithografie 37 × 28

76 Iosif V. Gerasimovič
(1893–1986)
Salamandra/Regie: G. Ročal,
Co-Regie: M. Doller,
Kamera: L. Forest'e, Ausstattung:
V. Egorov, Gemeinschafts-
produktion: Mečrabpom Film
und Prometheus
SU Lithografie 120 × 87

77 Richard Schwarzkopf
(1893 – vermutlich 1956)
Düsseldorf 1926/Grosse Ausstellung für Gesundheitspflege
sociale Fürsorge und Leibesübungen – Duesseldorf on Rhine/
Great German Exhibition 1926
Hygiene Social Assistance Sport
DE Linoldruck 195 × 90,5

78 Anonym
Palace Lawn Tennis Club
St. Moritz/Grand Tournoi Inter-
national – Grand International
Tournament
CH Lithografie 128 × 90,5

79 Eric de Coulon
(1888–1956, CH)
Blanc/au bon marché – Weiss-
waren/au bon marché – Whites
/au bon marché
1927
FR Lithografie 94 × 129

80 Anonym
Die Arbeit des 7. Kongresses der
Gewerkschaften der UdSSR,
Dezember 1926/Unsere Losung:
näher zu den Massen. Wir gingen
bis jetzt auf dem Wege Lenins
und werden auf ihm weitergehen
– The work of the 7th USSR Trade
Unions's Congress, December
1926/Our solution: closer to the
masses. We have come so far
on the path of Lenin and we shall
continue along that way
SU Lithografie 68 × 106

81 Ernst Böhm (1890–1963)
Grande Exposition Policière Berlin
1926 – Grosse Polizeiausstellung
– Grand Police Exhibition
DE Hochdruck 94 × 63

82 Otto Baumberger (1889–1961)
Ausverkauf Teppichhaus
Forster & Co – Carpet sale by
Forster & Co
CH Lithografie 127 × 90

83 Helmuth Kurtz (1903–1959)
Völkerkundliche Ausstellung
der Basler Mission – Basel
Mission Ethnological Exhibition
CH Hochdruck 90 × 64

84 Hubert Saget (1890–1949)
Forta/le ruban de cheveux
indéchirable – das unverwüstliche
Haarband – the indestructible
hair-ribbon
CH Lithografie 127 × 90

85 Antoon Kurvers (1889–1940)
Tentoonstelling van Neder-
landsche Gemeente Werken te
Utrecht –
Exhibition of Dutch Municipal
Works in Utrecht
NL Linoldruck 100 × 80

86 Cassandre [Adolphe
Jean-Marie Mouron] (1901–1968)
Ernest/Barcelona
FR Lithografie 120 × 80

87 Leonetto Cappiello
(1875–1942)
Acqua minerale naturale
San Bernardo/La più leggera
del mondo – Mineralwasser
San Bernardo/das leichteste der
Welt – San Bernardo mineral
water/the lightest in the world
IT Lithografie 140 × 100

88 Eric de Coulon (1888–1956)
Neuchâtel Plage – Strandbad –
Beach
ca. 1925
CH Lithografie 128 × 90,5

89 Jean-Gabriel Domergue
(1889–1961)
Alice Soulié
1926
FR Lithografie 160 × 119

90 André Daudé (1897–1979)
Pianos Daudé/sonorité
remarquable – Daudé
Klaviere/ausserordentliche
Klangfülle – Daudé pianos/
remarkable sonority
FR Lithografie
158 × 120

91 Emil Cardinaux (1877–1936)
Bally Schuhe – Bally shoes
CH Lithografie 127 × 90

Bibliografie / Bibliography

Die Bibliografie enthält eine Auswahl von Publikationen, die sich mit Fragen der Werbung und Plakatgestaltung befassen und die ausschliesslich im Jahr 1926 erschienen sind. Sie fördert also nicht im akademischen Sinne das Verständnis des Jahres 1926, sondern darf als Oberfläche, als atmosphärische Materialsammlung dessen angesehen werden, was die Grafiker, Typografen und «Reklame-Chefs», wie sie sich damals nannten, im Jahr 1926 beschäftigte.

The bibliography contains a selection of publications dealing with questions of advertising and poster design; they were all published in 1926. Thus the bibliography is not an aid to understanding the year 1926 in an academic sense, but may be seen as a surface view, as an atmospheric material collection of issues that graphic designers, typographers and "advertising bosses", as they were then known, were addressing in 1926.

Afficheur, L' (vermutlich Dermée, Paul), «Les belles affiches de France», in: *La Publicité,* Nr. 215–217 und 219–221, Paris, Januar–Juli 1926.

Albers, Josef, «Zur Ökonomie der Schriftform», in: *Offset- Buch- und Werbekunst,* Heft 7, Leipzig 1926, S. 395–397.

Allison, J. Murray, *First Essays on Advertising,* London 1926.

Andrin, Pierre, «Les maîtres d'hier et d'aujourd'hui: A. M. Cassandre», in: *L'Affiche,* Nr. 24, Paris, Dezember 1926, S. 151–155.

Anonym, «Die fascistische Gefahr», in: *Senefelder, Organ des Schweizerischen Lithographenbundes,* Nr. 15, Bern, 24. Juli 1926.

Bates, Charles Austin, «Take the Elevator to Success», in: *Printed Salesmanship,* Bd. 47, Cambridge, Mass., März 1926, S. 33–34.

Baumeister, Willy, «Neue Typographie», in: *Die Form,* Heft 10, Berlin 1926, S. 215–217.

Baur, Albert, «Schweizer Plakatsäulen», in: *Gebrauchsgraphik,* Nr. 7, Berlin 1926, S. 73–78.

Bayer, Herbert, «Versuch einer neuen Schrift», in: *Offset- Buch- und Werbekunst,* Heft 7, Leipzig, April 1926, S. 398–400.

Behne, Adolf, «Kultur, Kunst und Reklame», in: *Das Neue Frankfurt,* Heft 3, Frankfurt 1926/27, S. 57–60.

Bogačev, A., Plakat, Leningrad, 1926.

Brodskij, M., *Kak sdelat' plakat – losung – deklaraciju v izbe-čital'ne,* Leningrad 1926.

Buchartz, Max, «handschrift-type – zeichnung-foto», in: *Gebrauchsgraphik,* Nr. 8, Berlin 1926, S. 37–68.

Buchartz, Max, «Neuzeitliche Werbung», in: *Die Form,* Heft 7, Berlin, April 1926, S.136–140.

Chéronnet, Louis, «L'Art dans la rue», in: *L'Art vivant,* Nr. 25, Paris, Januar 1926, S. 20–25.

Dupuy, R.-L., «Quelques réflexions sur la publicité humoristique», in: *Vendre,* Nr. 30, Paris, April 1926, S. 353.

Fischer, Hugo, «Wirtschaftliche Kultur und Reklamekunst», in: *Offset- Buch- und Werbekunst,* Heft 2, Leipzig 1926, S. 77–79.

Frenzel, H.K., «Philadelphia die Stadt des 22. Kongesses der Vereinigten Reklameklubs der Welt», in: *Gebrauchsgraphik,* Nr. 10, Berlin 1926, S. 10–15.

Frenzel, H.K., «Die 22. Jahresversammlung der Vereinigten Reklameklubs der Welt», in: *Gebrauchsgraphik,* Nr. 10, Berlin 1926, S.17–22.

Frenzel, H.K., «Zur Methode der Amerikanischen Reklame», in: *Gebrauchsgraphik,* Nr. 10, Berlin 1926, S. 81–82.

Frenzel, H.K., «Deutsche Graphiker als ‹Freshmen› in Amerika», in: *Gebrauchsgraphik,* Nr. 11, Berlin 1926, S. 49–70.

Frenzel, H.K. (Hg.), *Ludwig Hohlwein,* Berlin 1926.

Giedion, Sigfried, «Ende und Neugestaltung der ‹Kunstgewerbeschulen›», in: *Neue Zürcher Zeitung,* Zürich 29. August 1926.

Gubler, F.T., «Der Wettbewerb des Schweizerischen Werkbundes zur Erlangung von Entwürfen für Leuchtplakatsäulen», in: *Das Werk,* Nr. 6, Zürich 1926, S. 193–194.

Hayne, Pet, «Wie Florida ‹gemacht› wurde – Die Geschichte eines Boom», in: *Offset- Buch- und Werbekunst,* Heft 5, Leipzig 1926, S. 254–260.

Hayne, Pet, «Die Sensation der Reklame», in: *Offset- Buch- und Werbekunst,* Heft 6, Leipzig 1926, S. 306–314.

Hellwag, Fritz, «Die Werbung für Bäder, Kurorte und Sommerfrischen», in: *Gebrauchsgraphik,* Nr. 7, Berlin 1926, S. 39–42.

Jones, Sindey R., Posters & Publicity, Fine Printing and Design, Special Autumn Number of *The Studio,* London 1926.

Jost, Heinrich, «Plakatkunst in der Schweiz», in: *Gebrauchsgraphik,* Nr. 7, Berlin 1926, S. 17–24.

Kassák, Lajos, «Die Reklame», in: *Das Werk,* Heft 7, Zürich, Juli 1926, S. 226–228.

Knickerbacker, Davis Leicester, «Does Your Advertising Talk as Well as It Looks?», in: *Printed Salesmanship,* Bd. 47, Cambridge, Mass., August 1926, S. 535–539.

König, Theodor, *Reklame-Psychologie – Ihr gegenwärtiger Stand – ihre praktische Bedeutung,* München, Berlin 1926 (erste Ausgabe 1924).

Kraszna-Krausz, Andor, «Wendung in der Kino-Plakat-Kunst!», in: *Filmtechnik,* Nr. 4, S. 77–78.

Krauss, Maximilian, «Deutsche Verkehrspropaganda»,
in: *Gebrauchsgraphik,* Nr. 9, Berlin 1926, S. 33–38.

Kropff, Hanns, *Wie werde ich Reklame-Chef?,* Wien 1926.

Lore, J.C.S., «Die Reklame auf den Hoch- und
Untergrund-Bahnen Berlins», in: *Gebrauchsgraphik,*
Nr. 9, Berlin 1926, S. 3–32.

Mataja, Viktor, *Die Reklame – Eine Untersuchung
über das Ankündigungswesen im Geschäftsleben,*
Leipzig 1926 (erste Auflage 1909).

Moholy-Nagy, László, «Fotoplastische Reklame»,
in: *Offset- Buch- und Werbekunst,* Heft 7, Leipzig,
April 1926, S. 386–394.

Molzahn, Johannes, «Ökonomie der Reklame-
Mechane», in: *Die Form,* Heft 7, Berlin, April 1926,
S. 141–145.

Ochocinskij, V., *Plakat. Razvitie i primenenie,*
Leningrad 1926.

Paneth, Erwin, *Entwicklung der Reklame vom Altertum
bis zur Gegenwart. Erfolgreiche Mittel der Gesellschafts-,
Personen- und Ideenreklame aus allen Zeiten und
Ländern,* München 1926.

Pauli, Fritz, *Plakat-Eichung, Wie man werbewirksam
Plakate auswählt,* Berlin, Hamburg, 1926.

Randolph, B.W., «Amerikanische Universitätsausbildung
in Reklame und Marktkunde», in: *Gebrauchsgraphik,*
Heft 2, Berlin 1926, S. 2–7.

Schwarz, Arthur, «Das neue russische Plakat»,
in: *Gebrauchsgraphik,* Nr. 7, Berlin 1926, S. 35–40.

Treskow, von, «Das Plakat der Polizeiausstellung»,
in: *Gebrauchsgraphik,* Nr. 9, Berlin 1926, S. 43–50.

Verneuil, M.P., «L'enseignement de l'art décoratif
dans l'urss», in: *Art et Décoration,* Bd. 49, Paris,
Januar–Juli 1926, S. 151–157.

W., «Eröffnung des Bauhauses Dessau», in: *Das Neue
Frankfurt,* Nr. 1, Frankfurt, Oktober/November 1926,
S. 44.

Weaver, Lawrence, «Die Funktionen eines Reklame-
Agenten», in: *Gebrauchsgraphik,* Nr. 11, Berlin 1926,
S. 41–48.

Wieynick-Dresden, Heinrich, «Neueste Wege
der Typographie», in: *Archiv für Buchgewerbe und
Gebrauchsgraphik,* Bd. 63, Heft 6, Leipzig 1926,
S. 373–382.

Wolff, W.H., «Belgische Warenhaus-Affichen»,
in: *Gebrauchsgraphik,* Nr. 7, Berlin 1926, S. 61–62

Hans Ulrich Gumbrecht, geboren 1928 in Würzburg, ist seit 1989 der Albert Guérard Professor of Literature im Department of Comparative Literature an der Stanford University und Professeur Associé am Département de Littérature Comparée de l'Université de Montréal. Zwischen 1971 und 1989 hat er an den Universitäten in Konstanz, Bochum und Siegen gelehrt. Seine Arbeitsgebiete sind die Geschichten der romanischen Literaturen und – derzeit – die philosophische Ästhetik. 1926 wurde sein Vater in einem unterfränkischen Dorf eingeschult – und bis er das Buch über 1926 zu schreiben begann, glaubte er, dass seine Grossmutter mütterlicherseits 1926 in Dortmund-Hörde an Kindbettfieber und sein Grossvater väterlicherseits im selben Jahr an den Folgen einer Kriegsverletzung gestorben seien.

Felix Studinka, geboren 1965 in Zürich. Seit 1997 Kurator der Plakatsammlung des Museums für Gestaltung Zürich. Seine Grosseltern väterlicherseits haben am 16. Februar 1926 in Budapest geheiratet. Der Grossvater mütterlicherseits war damals Student im belgischen Löwen und seine künftige Frau eine Schülerin in Antwerpen, die 1926 eine Revolte in der Ecole des Sœurs de Notre Dame auslöste, weil sie dafür bestraft worden war, im Schulhof flämisch gesprochen zu haben.

Hans Ulrich Gumbrecht, born in Würzburg in 1928, has been Albert Guérard Professor of Literature in the Department of Comparative Literature at Stanford University and Professeur Associé in the Département de Littérature Comparée de l'Université de Montréal since 1989. He taught at the universities of Konstanz, Bochum and Siegen from 1971 to 1989. He works in the fields of Romance literature and – at the time of writing – philosophical aesthetics. His father started work in a school in a village in Lower Franconia in 1926 – and until he started to write his book about 1926 he believed that his maternal grandmother died of puerperal fever in Hörde, Dortmund in 1926, and that his paternal grandfather died in the same year as the result of a war wound.

Felix Studinka, born 1965 in Zurich. Since 1997 curator of the Poster Collection at the Museum für Gestaltung Zürich. His paternal grandparents married on 16 February 1926 in Budapest. His maternal grandfather was a student in Leuven in Belgium at the time and his future wife was at school in Antwerp. In 1926, she unintentionally triggered a school revolt in the Ecole des Sœurs de Notre Dame because she had been punished for speaking Flemish in the school yard.

«Poster Collection»
Herausgegeben von/Published by
Museum für Gestaltung Zürich
Plakatsammlung/Poster Collection
Verantwortlich für die Publikationsreihe/
Responsible for the series of publications
Felix Studinka, Kurator/Curator
Bettina Richter, Wissenschaftliche Mitarbeiterin/
Scientific collaborator
Christina Reble, Publikationen/Publications
Museum für Gestaltung Zürich

Revue 1926
Herausgeber/Editor: Felix Studinka
Redaktion, Bildauswahl/Editing, picture selection:
Christina Reble, Felix Studinka
Lektorat/Sub-editing: Karin Schneuwly
Übersetzung/Translation: Michael Robinson, London
Gestaltung/Design: Integral Lars Müller, Matilda Plöjel
Lithografie/Repro: Ast & Jakob AG, Köniz
Druck/Printing: Vetsch + Co AG, Köniz
Einband/Binding: Buchbinderei Burkhardt AG,
Mönchaltorf

Museum für Gestaltung Zürich
Plakatsammlung/Poster Collection
Limmatstrasse 57
CH-8005 Zürich/Switzerland
e-mail: plakat.sammlung@museum-gestaltung.ch
http://www.museum-gestaltung.ch

Lars Müller Publishers
CH-5401 Baden/Switzerland
e-mail: books@lars-muller.ch

ISBN 3-907078-52-7
Erste Auflage/First Edition 2001

Printed in Switzerland